MOM - THIS JOKE'S FOR YOU

MOM - THIS JOKE'S FOR YOU

THE BEST MOM JOKES
FROM THE FUNNIEST COMEDIANS

edited by
JUDY BROWN

RONNIE SELLERS gift books PORTLAND, MAINE

Acknowledgements

*First of all, I'd like to thank all those professionally
funny people — the comedians — who have shared their
wit and wisdom about parenting.
And then, of course, I must thank the people
who raise the children of this world.*

Judy Brown

Published by Ronnie Sellers Productions, Inc.

Series Editor: Robin Haywood
Production Editor: Mary Baldwin
Designer: George Corsillo, Design Monsters

P.O. Box 818, Portland, Maine 04104
For ordering information:
Phone: 1-800-MAKE-FUN (800-625-3386)
Fax: (207) 772-6814
Visit our Web site: www.makefun.com
E-mail: rsp@rsvp.com

ISBN: 1-56906-583-7
Library of Congress Control Number: 2004094752

Introduction

Ah, motherhood. It's eternal — and inescapable.
We all have a mother. Many of us are mothers, or will be one.

Scientists have discovered that by the time a child reaches
nursery school age, he or she will laugh about 300 to 400 times
a day, while adults laugh only an average of 10 to 15 times.

The point of this book, Mom, is to help
you even up those odds.

Have fun,

Judy Brown
judybrowni@usa.net

Section ①

Moms to be
. . . or not to be

At the mall I saw a kid on a leash. And I think if I ever have a kid, it's gonna be cordless.

—WENDY LIEBMAN

I know lots of women who have had children. But I'm not sure it's for me. "Feel the baby kicking, feel the baby kicking," says my friend who is deliriously happy about it. To me, life is tough enough without having someone kick you from the inside.

—RITA RUDNER

If I ever have a kid I'm definitely going to breast-feed it, because I don't know how to cook. I would be breast-feeding him through college. His friends will be jealous.

—WENDY LIEBMAN

It would seem that something that means poverty, disorder, and violence every single day should be avoided entirely, but the desire to beget children is a natural urge.

—PHYLLIS DILLER

I adopted a baby. I wanted a highway, but it was a lot of red tape.

—MARGARET SMITH

I can't decide if I want a baby. And my friends who have kids don't make very good salesmen. They're like, "Oh you learn all this great stuff, like how to survive on two hours sleep." If I want to learn that, I'll just become a political prisoner or something.

—CATHRYN MICHON

I'd like to have kids. I get those maternal feelings. Like when I'm lying on the couch and I can't reach the remote control.

—KATHLEEN MADIGAN

I don't think I'll ever have a mother's intuition.
My sister left me alone in a restaurant with my
10-month-old nephew. I said, "What do I do if he
cries?" She said, "Give him some vegetables."
It turns out jalapeño is not his favorite.

—JANINE DITULLIO

I'm trying to decide whether or not to have
children. My time is running out. I know I want
to have children while my parents are still young
enough to take care of them.

—RITA RUDNER

I want to get married and have a lot of kids. I figure the more wage-earning people I bear, the better my chances are of someday getting into a really good nursing home.

—BRENDA PONTIFF

I'll be a real good mother. I've been called one.

—WENDY LIEBMAN

I've always had pets. I know I should have a child someday, but I wonder, could I love something that doesn't go in a box?

—SHEILA WENZ

I became a mom six months ago. I adopted a highway. I'm trying to teach it to pick up after itself.

—NANCY JO PERDUE

Artificial insemination. That's a scary concept. You know why? I don't want to have coffee with a stranger, never mind have their child.

—ROSIE O'DONNELL

I was asking my friend who has children, "What if I have a baby and I dedicate my life to it and it grows up to hate me. And it blames everything wrong with its life on me." And she said, "What do you mean, '*If*?'"

—RITA RUDNER

Surrogate mothers make me wonder: when is the right time to ask someone if you can borrow their uterus? Probably not right after you realize you didn't return their lawn mower.

—CYNDI STILES

In this day and age women can have kids for other women through surrogate motherhood. Is this the ultimate favor or what? I think I'm a good friend; I'll help you move. But what ever comes out of me after nine months, I'm keeping. I don't care if it's a shoe.

—SUE KOLINSKY

I'll never have a baby because I'm afraid I'll leave it on top of my car.

—LIZZ WINSTEAD

Section ②

They call it labor for a reason

Having a baby is definitely a labor of love.

—JOAN RIVERS

Did you have natural childbirth? Why? Do you have natural brain surgery or natural dentistry? I had a Jewish delivery: they knocked me out at the first pain and didn't wake me up until the hairdresser showed.

—JOAN RIVERS

What they put women through today when they're having a baby. They don't want to medicate them, as compared to previous generations. When my mom had me, she had so much medication she didn't wake up till I was seven.

—DENNIS WOLFBERG

My sister was in labor for 36 hours. Ouch. She got wheeled out of delivery, looked at me, and said, "Adopt."

—CAROLINE RHEA

I envy the kangaroo. That pouch setup is extraordinary; the baby crawls out of the womb when it is about two inches long, gets into the pouch, and proceeds to mature. I'd have a baby if it would develop in my handbag.

—RITA RUDNER

I had a baby. I said to my husband, "Honey, it's time," and my husband, a cautious man who usually doesn't rush, got from our house to the hospital in five minutes. Then he had to go back and get me.

—JEAN CARROLL

If you don't yell during labor, you're a fool. I screamed. Oh, how I screamed. And that was just during the conception.

—JOAN RIVERS

I want to have children, but my friends scared me. One of them told me she was in labor for thirty-six hours. I don't even want to do anything that feels *good* for thirty-six hours.

—RITA RUDNER

We planned this beautiful, totally natural, no-medications delivery. What kind of stupid-ass idea is that? Next time I want the epidural at the moment of conception. Numb for nine months.

—HEIDI JOYCE

I was born by cesarean section. This was the last time I had my mother's complete attention.

—RICHARD JENI

I don't get no respect. When I was born, the doctor smacked my mother.

—RODNEY DANGERFIELD

Mothers love to show those ugly Polaroid pictures of the child at one-hour old. I'm just glad they're free. They should be, they made my child look like a pit bull. Now I know where the *Enquirer* gets those weird alien pictures.

—SINBAD

That's how men participate now: they come into the room and say, "Breathe." Is that really sharing the experience? If I ever have a baby I want my husband to be on the table next to me, at least getting his legs waxed.

—RITA RUDNER

When the doctor asked me if I wanted a bikini cut for my cesarean section, I said, "No! A bikini and a wine cooler are why I'm lying here now."

—KIM TAVARES

A lucky woman in Iowa delivered seven babies. Ooh, that is not a delivery — that, my friends, is a shipment! For the parents, it's a dream — or a nightmare. Doesn't make any difference, either way they're never going to sleep again.

—DAVID LETTERMAN

Don't tell your kids you had an easy birth or they won't respect you. For years I used to wake up my daughter and say, "Melissa, you ripped me to shreds. Now go back to sleep."

—JOAN RIVERS

When my daughter was born, we videotaped the birth. Now when she makes me angry, I just hit rewind and put her back in.

—GRACE WHITE

I'm a new mother of two, and no, they're not twins. There's a medical term for a mother who gives birth to two babies in two years: suicidal.

—SUNDA CROONQUIST

When I gave birth, I had twins: my daughter and my husband. They were both immature and bald.

—GRACE WHITE

People are giving birth underwater now. They say it's less traumatic for the baby because it's in water. But certainly more traumatic for the other people in the pool.

—ELAYNE BOOSLER

This is exciting. A woman recently had a baby from an embryo that had been frozen for seven years. She said, "I had no idea if I was having a little boy, a little girl — or fish sticks."

—CONAN O'BRIEN

A mother's claim to your psyche is wholly substantiated because you love her. And you love her because she was your arrival terminal. She created you, so you always owe her and can never repay the debt. Being born is like asking Don Corleone a favor.

—DENNIS MILLER

I don't get no respect. My mother had morning sickness after I was born.

—RODNEY DANGERFIELD

Section ③

Mommy dearest

I just went for my annual physical and the doctor told me to take a stress test. So I called my mother.

—CRAIG SHARF

The way I feel, if the kids are still alive when my husband comes home from work, I've done my job.

—ROSEANNE

Most children threaten at times to run away from home. This is the only thing that keeps some parents going.

—PHYLLIS DILLER

A child of one can be taught not to do certain things, such as don't touch a hot stove, don't pull lamps off of tables, and don't wake Mommy before noon.

—JOAN RIVERS

I was one of the luckier women, I came to motherhood with some experience. I owned a Yorkshire terrier for three years. At 10 months, my children could stay and heel. At a year, they could catch a Frisbee in their teeth in midair. At 15 months, after weeks of rubbing their noses in it and putting them outside, they were paper-trained.

—ERMA BOMBECK

We spend the first twelve months of our children's lives teaching them to walk and talk and the next twelve telling them to sit down and shut up.

—PHYLLIS DILLER

My mother never breast-fed me. She told me that she only liked me as a friend.

—RODNEY DANGERFIELD

My mom breast-fed me but it was only 2%.

—WENDY LIEBMAN

It ain't easy being me. My mother breast-fed me through a straw.

—RODNEY DANGERFIELD

When I was a kid I got no respect. I told my mother, "I'm gonna run away from home." She said, "On your mark . . ."

—RODNEY DANGERFIELD

I hate changing my baby's diapers after he poops. I know exactly what he ate at daycare. Yesterday, it was carrots. Tomorrow I'm hoping for long-stem roses.

—SHIRLEY LIPNER

I was a mouthy child and when my mother had enough she'd say, "Come sit on my lap, and we'll look up orphanages." Sure, it's funny now.

—JACKIE KASHIAN

I grew up hearing such stupid things. My mother would say, "That's the last time I'm gonna tell you to take out the garbage." Well, thank God.

—GEORGE WALLACE

Before my mother would give you that dime allowance, she'd want you to do a little chore around the house. Like build a porch.

—RAY ROMANO

My parents were both in the Marine Corps. But I had a pretty normal upbringing: I stood guard duty all night just like all kids. And my mom made me wash the bathroom floor with a toothbrush, so I used hers.

—MARY GALLAGHER

My mom taught me everything I needed to know. Don't talk to strangers, don't pay retail, and the size of your hair should always match the size of your ass.

—STEPHANIE SCHIERN

Once I was riding my bike and my mom was waving to me from her bedroom window. She said, "Judy, soon your body will change." I said, "I know, like in puberty." She said, "No, that Good Humor truck."

—JUDY GOLD

My mother's house: exposed bricks and nerves.
She lives in a predominantly anxious part
of town.

—RICHARD LEWIS

My mother has gossip dyslexia. She has to talk in
front of people's backs.

—RICHARD LEWIS

In my family, everyone is seeing a psychologist,
except my mother. She creates the patients.

—STEPHANIE SCHIERN

I have two kids, and over the years I've developed a really relaxed attitude about the whole child-rearing thing. I don't cry over spilt milk. Spilt vodka, that's another story.

—DARRYL HOGUE

My four-year-old pissed me off last night when he woke me at 5 a.m. and wouldn't go back to sleep. Oh well, otherwise I might have missed out on ordering that child-rearing video by Joan Crawford.

—LIZ SELLS

My mother wrapped the living room furniture in plastic. We practiced safe-sitting in our household.

—ADAM FERRARA

An answering machine is like the stupidest gift to give your parents. No one ever calls them except for their kids. My mother put the appropriate message on the machine: "Look, we're not here right now. If you'd like to leave a message, leave one. If you don't want to leave one, don't. We're not going to be making decisions for you anymore. So make up your own goddamn mind. Thank you."

—JUDY GOLD

My mom always says, "Keep your chin up."
That's how I ran into the door.

—DARYL HOGUE

My family is so dysfunctional that when I looked
up the word "dysfunctional" in the dictionary
there was a picture of my mother.

—PAULA R. HAWKINS

My mother always said, "Don't marry for money.
Divorce for money."

—WENDY LIEBMAN

When I was little I asked my mother, "Do you love me?" She said "I love you when you're sleeping." When I was 14, I asked, "Mom, am I ugly?" She said, "It's OK, when you're 16 you can get a nose job." When I was leaving for school, she said, "I don't know why we're spending any money to send you to college, you don't deserve it." When I came home for Mother's Day, she asked, "Where's my present?" I said, "Your present is: I still only have one personality, and it's not planning to kill you!"

—ROBIN ROBERTS

Saw my mom today. It was all right, she didn't see me.

—MARGARET SMITH

My mom is always on the prowl trying to find potential suitors for me, but she's gone over the edge. My brother had a little fender bender, and my mom was trying to set me up with all the men at the scene of the accident. "What about the cop?" "No, Mom." "The tow truck guy?" "Mom!" "What about the guy who hit your brother?" "He was driving drunk!" "You're so quick to judge people."

—LORI GIARNELLA

My mother is 60, and her whole life she only slept with one guy. She won't tell me who.

—WENDY LIEBMAN

My mother was 88 years old. She never used glasses. Drank right out of the bottle!

—HENNY YOUNGMAN

My mom wanted to know why I never get home for the holidays. I said, "Because I can't get Delta to wait in the yard while I run in."

—MARGARET SMITH

My mom is very possessive. She calls me up and says, "You weren't home last night. Is something going on?" I said, "Yeah, Mom. I'm cheating on you with another mother."

—HEIDI JOYCE

My mother complained about her order in a restaurant and tried to send it back. I had to stop her, "Ma, you can't send back food after you've finished eating it!"

—ROBERTA ROCKWELL

I like to talk to my mother every single day, because hearing how delusional I may become makes me appreciate every day that I have left with my sanity.

—TAMI VERNEKOFF

Last year I left my job to stay home with my kids. One nice thing about it is, I'm my own boss. So I declared "Real Casual" Fridays. I don't get out of bed.

—EILEEN COURTNEY

Section ④

When I'm in my grave, you'll be sorry

Therapy is like a really easy game show where the answer to every question is: "My mom?"

—ROBIN GREENSPAN

My mother could make anybody feel guilty. She used to get letters of apology from people she didn't even know.

—JOAN RIVERS

My mother is so passive-aggressive. She says things to me like, "You just can't seem to do anything right, and that's what I really love about you."

—LAURA SILVERMAN

My mother just wrote her autobiography. Pick it up. It's in the stores right now. It's entitled, *I Came, I Saw, I Criticized*.

—JUDY GOLD

I got on the phone, my mom said, "Hi! Is everything wrong?"

—RICHARD LEWIS

You may view yourself as a mature, self-reliant person, but your mom views you as a person who once got lost in the department store and got so scared that you pooped your pants. Which caused you to become so ashamed that you tried to hide in the ladies lingerie department where the nice clerk was able to find you because she noticed the highly unromantic aroma emanating from somewhere inside a rack of negligees.

—DAVE BARRY

My mother was a ventriloquist. She could throw her voice. So for ten years I thought the dog was telling me to kill my father.

—WENDY LIEBMAN

When I was 12, I went as my mother for Halloween. I put on a pair of heels, went door to door, and criticized what everyone else was wearing.

—ROBIN BACH

When I miss my mom and her guilt trips, I watch PBS pledge breaks.

—BONNIE CHEESEMAN

My mother is a typical Jewish mother. They sent her home from jury duty, she insisted she was guilty.

—CATHY LADMAN

My mother's house: the Sufferdome.

—RICHARD LEWIS

I'm Catholic. My mother and I were unpacking and she found my diaphragm. I had to tell her it was a bathing cap for my cat.

—LIZZ WINSTEAD

Why did Mom insist on cutting my hair herself until I was 14? She had a home haircut kit that looked like Mengele's briefcase and the barber skills of Dr. Leatherface brandishing a Flowbee.

—DENNIS MILLER

When my mother makes out her income tax return every year, under Occupation, she writes in, "Eroding my daughter's self-esteem."

—ROBIN ROBERTS

When we were growing up my mother told my brother he was a pain in the neck. He became a chiropractor. I'm glad she didn't call him a pain in the ass.

—JOEL WARSHAW

For the holidays I bought my mother a self-complaining oven.

—RICHARD LEWIS

Every time I did something bad, my mother would say, "How could you? After all the sacrifices I've made for you." And she did, once a week she would kill a chicken in front of my photograph.

—JOAN RIVERS

My mother calls at 5:30 in the morning. I'm not a dairy farm. I don't like phone calls before six in the morning.

—RICHARD LEWIS

My mom, she wakes me at six in the morning and says, "The early bird catches the worm." If I want a worm, Mom, I'll drink a bottle of tequila.

—PAM STONE

My mother and I had different attitudes toward sex. She said, "Whatever you do, never sleep with a man until he buys you a house." Well, it worked for her, and I got a swing set out of the deal.

—JUDY BROWN

I'm trying to keep my mother from calling me every day. I moved 2,000 miles away, she calls me to tell me how high the phone bills are. My sister bought her a computer and taught her e-mail. So now my mother e-mails me and then calls me to tell me she sent me e-mail. If I respond, she calls me to tell me she got the response, and then keeps me on the phone for a half hour about what she just e-mailed. Instead of one call a day, I'm now getting 24 calls and 16 e-mails with the other eight or so calls along the line of, "Did it go through?" Yes, about 40 times. Stop pressing send. I had to report my mother for spam.

—MARIA MENOZZI

I told my mother that I was thinking about seeing a therapist. She thought that was a good idea because she heard they made a lot of money.

—DARLENE HUNT

My mother on The Dating Game, how great would that be? "Bachelor Number Two: We're at a dinner dance at the temple, I fall and break a hip, do you: A.) Stay with me on the dance floor, B.) Run and get help, C.) Leave me there to drop dead just like my kids would."

—JUDY GOLD

My mother always says, "If I ever get senile, just put me in a home. I don't want to be a burden to you." And I say, "Mom, I would shoot you dead before I would do that."

—LAURA SILVERMAN

Mothers stress the lovely meaning of Mother's Day by gathering their children and tenderly saying, "I carried every one of you in my body for nine months and then my hips started spreading because of you. I wasn't built like this until you were born and I didn't have this big blue vein in the back of my leg. You did this to me."

—BILL COSBY

My mother wasn't the protective type. When my father left, she told us kids, "Don't think this just had to do with me. Your father left all of us."

—CAROLINE RHEA

My mom taught me how to drive. I can't drive worth a damn, but I can change all my clothes at a stoplight.

—CRAIG SHOEMAKER

Domestic goddess

I'm a housewife, but I prefer to be called
a domestic goddess.

—ROSEANNE

Cleaning the house before your kids are done growing is like shoveling the walk before it stops snowing.

—PHYLLIS DILLER

You make the beds, you do the dishes, and six months later you have to start all over again

—JOAN RIVERS

My mother used to say, "You can eat off my floor." You can eat off my floor, too. There are thousands of things there.

—ELAYNE BOOSLER

Moms will clean up everything. Scientists have proven that a mom's spit is the exact chemical composition of Formula 409. Mom's spit on a Kleenex? You get rust off a bumper with that.

—JEFF FOXWORTHY

I'm not the least bit domestic, and I don't care.
We have a ring around the tub you could set a
drink on.

—PHYLLIS DILLER

What mother has never fallen on her knees when
she has gone into her son's bedroom and prayed,
"Please God, no more. You were only supposed
to give me what I could handle."

—ERMA BOMBECK

You never hear a kid say, "Do you want me to dust the baseboards?"

—ELLEN DEGENERES

Don't cook. Don't clean. No man will ever make love to a woman because she waxed the linoleum. "My God, the floor's immaculate. Lie down, you hot hussy."

—JOAN RIVERS

I buried a lot of my ironing in the back yard.

—PHYLLIS DILLER

My mother from time to time puts on her wedding dress. Not because she's sentimental. She just gets really far behind in her laundry.

—BRIAN KILEY

I hate doing laundry. I don't separate the colors from the whites. I put them together and let them learn from their cultural differences.

—RITA RUDNER

It is better to light just one candle, than to clean the whole apartment.

—EILEEN COURTNEY

I bought an electric broom, and my husband said, "Electric brooms are for lazy people. Why don't you use a regular one?" I'm not sure how well my new broom sweeps yet, but it sure works swell to beat a man over the head.

—STEPHANIE SCHIERN

Everything in my mother's house is for a special occasion that hasn't happened yet. My mother's waiting for the pope to show up for dinner to break out the good stuff. Or Tony Danza.

—RAY ROMANO

You never hear a kid say, "I should probably Scotchguard that."

—ELLEN DEGENERES

Why do they put lights on vacuum cleaners? To see the dirt? I don't want to see the dirt, that's why I vacuum.

—JEANNIE DIETZ

I never get tired of housework. I don't do any. When guests come to visit, I just put out drop cloths and say we're painting.

—JOAN RIVERS

I'm not going to vacuum until Sears makes one you can ride on.

—ROSEANNE

My mom is a neat freak. If she adopted a highway, she'd mop it once a week. She'd reroute traffic, "Don't drive on my clean freeway!"

—DANIEL LIEBERT

Housework can't kill you, but why take a chance?

—PHYLLIS DILLER

There's an old saying, "Neurotics build castles in the air, and psychotics live in them." My mother cleans them.

—RITA RUDNER

I love it when my husband thinks I might leave him. He gets so insecure, he does the dishes. Too bad I have to actually file divorce papers to get him to clean the toilet.

—SHIRLEY LIPNER

I was taking caring of myself before I got married, my husband was taking care of himself. I thought, let's just continue down this path. But he would come home and say stuff like, "What's for dinner?" I replied, "I don't know. What did you cook?" And one time he actually said this: "I'm all out of clean underwear." To which I replied, "Oh, then you need to do some wash. I did laundry yesterday, I got a drawer full of clean panties. You're welcome to borrow a pair to tide you over."

—WANDA SYKES

I've been so busy, I don't even have time to cook for my kids. I don't wanna say we eat out a lot, but I've noticed that lately when I call my kids for dinner they run to the car.

—JULIE KIDD

My ex-husband cheated on me, even though I was a good wife and mother; I cleaned, I cooked. The way to a man's heart may be through his stomach, but that's only if you twist the blade and lift up.

—SHEILA KAY

I got my sense of humor from my mother. When I was growing up, she refused to bake. She said, "Why, you'll just eat it."

—BETSY SALKIND

My mom was a little weird. When I was little, Mom would make chocolate frosting, and she'd let me lick the beaters. And then she'd turn them off.

—MARTY COHEN

The most remarkable thing about my mother is that for 30 years she served the family nothing but leftovers. The original meal has never been found.

—CALVIN TRILLIN

At Thanksgiving, my mom always makes too much food, especially one item, like 700 or 800 pounds of sweet potatoes. She's got to push it during the meal. "Did you get some sweet potatoes? There's sweet potatoes. They're hot. There's more in the oven, some more in the garage. The rest are at the Johnsons'."

—LOUIE ANDERSON

When it comes to food, my mother is neurotic. I tell my friends when they come over, "When you're done with the meal, my mother's going to try to give you more. If you want a little bit more, tell her, 'I'm full.' Boom, a little bit more. If you want a lot more, you tell her 'just a tiny bit.' Boom, another meal, just like that. But if you don't want any more at all, you have to shoot her."

—RAY ROMANO

Most turkeys taste better the day after. My mother's tasted better the day before.

—RITA RUDNER

I was so ugly, my mother used to feed me with a slingshot.

—RODNEY DANGERFIELD

I hate how my grocery store is always rearranging things. Product placement is what they call it. The other day I had just enough time to run in for a jar of spaghetti sauce and couldn't find it. But I learned something: my kids will eat peanut butter on anything. That night, we had Skippy fettucine.

—EILEEN COURTNEY

The cheapest thing my mother ever bought was the peanut butter with the jelly inside. Peanut butter with jelly in the same jar, how low can you go? That's like buying a shoe with a sock sewn inside.

—CHRIS ROCK

My mother had plastic slipcovers on the couch. When I was six years old, I put a ham sandwich in it. When I found it last week, it was still fresh.

—DANNY MCWILLIAMS

You want to hear the childhood daredevil stories my mother tells company? "Once a glass broke on the kitchen floor, not one week later my daughter was in there without her shoes on." I broke a glass in 1954, they sold the house in 1985, my mother warned the new owners. "I think I got all the big pieces, but there could be slivers."

—ELAYNE BOOSLER

OK, I admit it. I had a kid so I'd have an excuse to buy Marshmallow Fluff.

—CARYN LESCHEN

Mom– this joke's for you

I've been married fourteen years and I have
three kids. Obviously, I breed well in captivity.

—ROSEANNE

I had far too many kids. At one time in our playpen it was standing room only. It looked like a bus stop for midgets. It used to be so damp in there we had a rainbow above it.

—PHYLLIS DILLER

You don't know what love is until you become a parent. You don't know what love is until you fish a turd out of the bathtub for someone. And you have to be positive about it: "Good job!"

—MARGARET SMITH

The relationship between mothers and children never changes and that's because no matter how rich or powerful you are your mother still remembers when you were three and put Spaghetti-Os up your nose.

—DENNIS MILLER

Have you ever had a four-year-old tell you a joke? It takes about two hours, has no semblance or order, and you have to know when it's over.

—ROSIE O'DONNELL

When you have a baby, nobody ever checks to see if you're a good parent. When you adopt, they check. Those social services people drove me crazy. They called me every day, "You child-proof the house yet? You child-proof the house?" "Yeah, he'll never get in here."

—MARGARET SMITH

The most effective birth control I know is a toddler with the croup and diaper rash.

—KATE ZANNONI

You never know what you're going to get and children have their own personalities immediately. I was watching little kids on a carousel — some kids were jumping on the horses, some kids were afraid of the horses, some kids were betting on the horses.

—RITA RUDNER

I'm 43, and I have a two-year-old. And I did it on purpose, so you know I'm not that bright.

—STEPHANIE HODGE

I love being a mom. My four-year-old son tells me how pretty I am, that he loves me and wants to marry me. I love him, too, but I don't think he could support me in the style to which I'm accustomed. Not as a Power Ranger, anyway.

—LIZ SELLS

My mother loved children. She would have given anything if I had been one.

—GROUCHO MARX

I tell you there is no love sweeter than the love between a mother and a child. Now I know my wife loves me, but I am reasonably sure that she doesn't look at me the same way she looks at them. You know it's kind of humbling because you realize at some point you're just a date that worked out.

—DENNIS MILLER

The real menace in dealing with a five-year-old is that in no time at all you begin to sound like a five-year-old.

—JEAN KERR

My daughter was rubbing my legs, giving me a mommy massage. She said, "Mom, your skin is so soft." I thought, "Oh, how sweet." Then she said, "Soft like Play-Doh. I'm gonna make a dinosaur now, okay?"

—MEL FINE

My childhood was pretty bad. When I was seven, my mother told me I was selfish. One day I asked for dinner. "You're just like your father," she said.

—GLORIA BRINKWORTH

Before I became a mother I was such a free spirit. I used to say "No man will ever dominate me." Now I have a six-year-old master.

—SULLY DIAZ

When you're a kid, basically your mother's job is to make you look like a dork. The mittens pinned to your jacket, the Elmer Fudd earflap hat, the rubber boots with the Wonder bread bags over your feet, and of course, the piece de resistance, the snow pants. There's an outfit that just screams "Go ahead, beat the crap out of me and take my lunch money!"

—DENNIS MILLER

The way we know the kids are growing up: the bite marks are higher.

—PHYLLIS DILLER

Having kids around the house I realize the stupid things I say to them that my parents used to say to me. Like, "Stop making faces or you'll stay that way." I remember looking at one of my uncles thinking, "So that's what happened to him."

—MARIA MENOZZI

You get a lot of tension. You get a lot of headaches. I do what it says on the aspirin bottle: Take two and keep away from children.

—ROSEANNE

What's harder to raise, boys or girls? Girls. Boys are easy. Give 'em a book of matches and they're happy.

—ETTA MAY

Kids? It's like living with homeless people. They're cute but they just chase you around all day long going, "Can I have a dollar? I'm missing a shoe! I need a ride!"

—KATHLEEN MADIGAN

I've got three kids. I had one with the birth control pill, one with a diaphragm, and another with the IUD. I don't know what happened to my IUD, but I have my suspicions. That kid picks up HBO.

—ROSEANNE

Living with my daughters is like driving on the freeway. At first I'm optimistic, but gradually I'll just settle for no bloodshed.

—GLORIA BRINKWORTH

Kids are cute, babies are cute, puppies are cute. The little things are cute. See, nature did this on purpose so that we would want to take care of our young. Made them cute. Tricked us. Then gradually they get older and older, until one day your mother sits you down and says, "You know, I think you're ugly enough to get your own apartment."

—CATHY LADMAN